CHAPTER 1

NAVIGATING AUDIENCE SELECTION

Choosing the right audience is a vital component in the success of TikTok ad campaigns. This chapter sheds light on various audience selection mechanisms available on TikTok, enabling businesses to connect with their potential customers effectively.

Geographical & Linguistic Preferences

TikTok extends the ability to pinpoint an audience based on their geographical location and language preferences. This lets businesses reach out to people in specific countries, cities or even regions while also considering the language they are most comfortable with.

Interests & Preferences Determination

TikTok empowers businesses to select users who have a knack for certain areas of interest. This selection criterion leverages user data related to content consumption and platform interaction, aiding businesses in aligning their promotions with users who have shown a liking for similar content.

Audience Behavior Insights

One of the significant advantages of TikTok is its behavior-based targeting. It enables businesses to connect with audiences whose past platform interactions and engagements resonate with their offerings. This includes a user's history of engagement with different video content and accounts, and their interaction with past advertisements.

Custom Audience Configuration

TikTok extends the feature of custom audience targeting, which lets advertisers import their existing customer databases or other identifiers. TikTok matches the imported data with its user profiles, providing a way to specifically target existing customers or even create similar audience profiles.

Mirror Audience Identification

Mirror audience targeting is a unique feature where TikTok allows businesses to reach users who bear similarities with their existing customers. This involves utilizing the data from the custom audiences or tracking pixels, identifying users with similar traits, habits, and interests.

Re-engagement Strategy

TikTok's retargeting options enable businesses to re-engage with users who have had past interactions with their promotions or website. This enhances brand recall, encourages conversions, and boosts engagement with users who have previously shown interest.

Device & Platform Specifics

TikTok lets businesses fine-tune their ads for users using specific devices or operating systems. This feature is beneficial for businesses wishing to deliver a seamless ad experience across different device types or platforms.

Network Connection Orientation

TikTok provides options to target audiences based on their network connection type, such as Wi-Fi or cellular data. This feature aids in optimizing ad delivery based on the network capabilities of users.

Control Over Ad Positioning

Advertisers on TikTok have the power to choose their ad placements within the app. This feature ensures that ads are displayed in a context that maximizes their influence and impact.

Exclusion Criteria

In addition to defining target audiences, TikTok also offers exclusion options. Businesses can avoid specific demographics, interests, or behaviors from their target audience to prevent showing ads to uninterested or irrelevant users.

Engagement-based Selection

TikTok enables businesses to target users based on their engagement with specific TikTok content or accounts. It helps reach users who have previously shown a higher level of interest or activity on the platform.

Implementing TikTok Pixel

TikTok Pixel, when implemented on a website, helps businesses track user actions, conversions, and behaviors outside the TikTok platform. This data can be employed for retargeting efforts or creating custom audience segments based on specific user interactions.

Considering the target audience meticulously and opting for the most relevant audience selection mechanisms are crucial for effective advertising.
With the multitude of targeting options on TikTok, businesses can fine-tune their ad campaigns and deliver tailored and engaging content to their intended audience.

CHAPTER 2

DISCOVERING THE RICH TAPESTRY OF TIKTOK ADVERTISING

TikTok is the social media juggernaut of our time, known for its vibrant and varied user base. Its incredible ascent in the advertising space is a testament to the dynamism and creativity it offers. Let's delve into the diverse ad formats that TikTok provides marketers, each with a unique engagement strategy to effectively deliver your brand's message.

In-Feed Ads can be found tucked into the regular feed of TikTok videos. They create a seamless user experience as users swipe through their feed, with your ad presented as just another engaging TikTok video. With options for both visual and textual content, these ads can be up to a minute long, providing ample time to capture users' attention.

Brand Takeovers serve a high-impact ad right when users open the app, ensuring your brand is the first thing they see. This format leverages eye-catching graphics in the form of images, GIFs, or short videos and can be linked to any landing page of your choice.

Taking brand visibility a step further, TopView Ads provide brands an extended time slot to engage users. Placed in a premium location, they appear as the first in-feed video, offering room for detailed storytelling and user engagement.

Hashtag Challenges are a TikTok special, fostering user interaction by inviting them to create and share content using a branded hashtag. This innovative approach leads to a surge in user-generated content, bolstering brand awareness significantly.

Branded Effects bring an interactive twist to advertising. Users can utilize custom filters, stickers, and Augmented Reality (AR) effects in their videos, naturally incorporating your brand into their content.

Branded Hashtag Challenges PLUS offer a similar experience, with the added bonus of an in-app shopping feature. This allows users to discover and buy products, simplifying the user journey from product discovery to purchase.

The Custom Influencer Package is a unique partnership opportunity with popular TikTok creators. Brands can leverage an influencer's genuine rapport and substantial follower base to reach their target audience more authentically.

The Branded Effects AR Games provide users a unique gaming experience within the app, involving various branded elements, enhancing user engagement and creating deeper brand connections.

Branded Scan offers an exciting interaction with the real world. Users can scan physical objects using their TikTok camera, which activates branded filters or effects, creating an engaging blend of digital and physical experiences.

E-commerce Ads offer a seamless shopping experience within the app, allowing product displays and in-app purchases. This keeps users within the TikTok ecosystem, providing an uninterrupted shopping journey.

The Customized Ad Experiences provide bespoke interactions that can include interactive polls, quizzes, games, and more. These experiences enhance user engagement and make your brand memorable.

Finally, Dynamic Product Ads offer a highly personalized shopping experience. Based on user browsing history, these ads dynamically change product images, descriptions, and pricing, offering suggestions tailored to individual users.

As you sail the vast ocean of TikTok advertising, picking the right ad format can make or break your campaign. Be clear about your goals, understand your audience, and choose the ad format that will resonate most with the TikTok community.

CHAPTER 3

MASTERING THE ART OF CAPTIVATING AUDIENCES

Creating content that commands and sustains the attention of TikTok's dynamic user base is an art unto itself. Here are some unique tips to guide you in the design of impactful, engaging TikTok content:

Embrace the TikTok Beat: Every social media platform has its individual vibe, and TikTok is no different. To resonate with its specific audience, familiarize yourself with the platform's trends, celebrated challenges, and prevalent formats. Incorporating vibrant music, innovative transitions, and stunning visual effects can help your content mesh with TikTok's beat.

Spin a Story: Storytelling is a powerful tool on TikTok. Craft an engaging narrative that grips viewers from start to finish. Instead of following the traditional introduction-body-conclusion structure, consider taking your viewers on a riveting journey that sparks curiosity and suspense. Amplify your story with text overlays or voiceovers for an added punch.

Maximize the Short-Form: Although TikTok allows videos up to 60 seconds, clips that are shorter often attract more engagement. Strive for brevity, clearness, and sharpness in your content. A swift, dynamic rhythm can help retain viewers' interest.

Be Authentic and Accessible: TikTok users value genuineness. Rather than producing polished, overproduced videos, adopt a more natural, genuine approach.

Communicate with your audience in a friendly, everyday tone to establish a connection with them.

Inject Humor and Enjoyment: TikTok is a platform recognized for its fun, humorous content. Infusing a touch of humor into your videos can offer a joyful experience for viewers. Clever wordplay, visual comedy, or surprising twists can make your content irresistible and unforgettable.

Engage with Trends and Challenges: Participating in trending TikTok content can enhance your visibility and engagement. Stay updated with the latest hashtags, popular music, and trending challenges, and discover creative ways to blend your brand into them.

Deploy Enticing Visuals: High-definition visuals, striking colors, and captivating visual elements can make your content stand out on this visually-oriented platform. Experiment with diverse camera perspectives, transitions, and visual effects to create an intriguing viewing experience.

Foster Viewer Interaction: Design compelling call-to-action prompts to spur viewer engagement. Encourage viewers to like, share, comment, or follow your account, which can amplify your reach and boost the success of your TikTok campaign.

Learn, Adjust, and Enhance: Track the performance of your TikTok content and modify your strategies based on user reactions and engagement metrics. Embrace experimentation. Constant refinement is essential for an effective content strategy.

Capitalize on User Contributions: TikTok users appreciate user-generated content. Infuse elements of user involvement into your ads by initiating hashtag challenges, contests, or campaigns that motivate viewers to share their experiences with your brand.

Showcase Your Product: TikTok provides an exceptional platform to showcase your product in action. Generate content that highlights the unique features and advantages of your product in a visually engaging manner.

Collaborate with Influencers: Partnerships with influencers who resonate with your brand can increase your reach and strengthen your brand's credibility.

Engage Proactively: Respond to comments and inquiries, and acknowledge user-generated content related to your brand to cultivate a community atmosphere.

Inform and Enlighten: Distribute valuable content that provides insights, advice, or tutorials relevant to your industry. Utilize visual aids or step-by-step demonstrations to make your educational content engaging and easy to grasp.

Evoke Emotions: Trigger a range of emotions with your TikTok content to foster a deeper connection with viewers. Content that elicits emotions like humor, nostalgia, or inspiration can produce a memorable and shareable experience for viewers.

CHAPTER 4

MASTERING TIKTOK'S INFLUENCER OUTREACH

TikTok's influencer marketing can be a powerful tool for businesses seeking to connect with their potential consumers. With a vast community of influencers boasting considerable followings, this digital space offers an unmatched opportunity to captivate audiences. Here's your comprehensive guide to maximizing influencer outreach on TikTok:

Objective Setting: Clearly pinpoint your objectives prior to embarking on influencer marketing. Do you aim to amplify brand visibility, drive traffic to your website, boost sales, or spotlight a particular campaign? Understanding your goals paves the way to selecting the ideal influencers and gauging campaign success.

Spotting the Right Influencer: Target influencers who embody your brand ethos, cater to your intended audience, and fit within your campaign goals. Take into account factors such as their follower count, engagement rate, content quality, and audience demographics. TikTok's search tool, popular hashtags, and influencer marketing platforms could be your key to discovering the right influencers.

Ensuring Authenticity: Authenticity is a cornerstone of TikTok's appeal. Opt for influencers who demonstrate a genuine bond with their followers and whose content aligns with your brand and resonates with your target market. Scrutinize their engagement rates, comments, and the overall audience sentiment.

Reaching Out to Influencers: After identifying suitable influencers, approach them with an enticing proposal that lays out collaboration specifics including deliverables, timeline, compensation, and any specific directives.
Customize your proposal to reflect an understanding of the influencer's content style.

Fostering Collaborative Content: Work in tandem with influencers to create content that spotlights your brand or product in an engaging, authentic manner. Offer them key messaging pointers or creative directives, but allow them the artistic liberty to infuse their unique style and voice.

Tapping into Hashtag Challenges: Leverage the power of hashtag challenges to encourage user-generated content and ignite a viral campaign. Collaborate with influencers to initiate a branded hashtag challenge that prompts their followers to engage.

Measuring Impact: Set up tracking mechanisms to evaluate the success of your influencer marketing strategy. Monitor metrics like views, likes, comments, shares, and conversions. Use custom URLs, promotional codes, or trackable links to directly attribute conversions to influencer content.

Cultivating Long-Term Partnerships: Establishing enduring relationships with influencers can be advantageous for future campaigns and fostering brand loyalty. If an influencer's content strikes a chord with your audience and yields desired outcomes, consider extending the collaboration.

Adherence to FTC Guidelines: Ensure that your influencer marketing campaigns comply with the Federal Trade Commission (FTC) guidelines regarding sponsored content. Clearly disclose any partnerships or sponsorships within the influencer's content to uphold transparency and trust with the audience.

Experimenting with Collaboration Formats: Beyond sponsored content, consider challenge duets, or even influencer takeovers of your TikTok account.

Be receptive to innovative ideas and work alongside influencers to find the ideal format that serves your campaign goals.

Magnifying Influencer Content: Once your influencer has crafted and shared content featuring your brand, maximize that content across your own TikTok account and other social platforms. Repost and share the influencer's content, giving them proper acknowledgment.

Exploring Micro-Influencers: Micro-influencers, although possessing smaller followings, boast highly engaged and niche audiences. They often enjoy a more personal connection with their followers and can evoke higher levels of trust and authenticity.

Promoting User-Generated Content (UGC): Besides influencer content, encourage regular users to create and share their content related to your brand or campaign. Enlist influencers to incite their followers to participate in the creation of UGC.

CHAPTER 5

LEVERAGING SUCCESSFUL PRACTICES AND BOOSTING OUTCOMES

In the world of TikTok advertising, the path to successfully achieving your goals and enhancing ROI is paved with astute measurement of outcomes and strategic optimization. Following are novel approaches to ensure the efficacy and impact of your TikTok advertisement crusades:

Constructing Success Indices: Aligning your campaign aspirations with specifically outlined success indices like impressions, interaction ratios, conversion rates, or brand perception metrics can play a crucial role. Establishing these indices facilitates campaign efficacy measurement and progress tracking.

Harnessing the Power of TikTok's Analytics Dashboard: TikTok offers a potent platform, its Analytics Dashboard, to monitor campaign outcomes. It serves as a real-time, comprehensive overview of your campaign performance, enabling a deeper understanding of areas requiring enhancement and elements fueling your success.

Championing the Art of Split Testing: Comparing and contrasting different advertisement variants via split testing offers valuable insights. It involves experimenting with creative components, advertisement formats, captions, or audience targeting options to discover the most effective combination. Split your audience base into distinct subsets and compare their reactions to fine-tune your strategy.

Capturing Conversions: Establish conversion tracking parameters to quantify the tangible impact of your ads on specific targets like website traffic, sign-ups, purchases. Leveraging trackable URLs, pixel monitoring, or custom event tracking to link conversions back to your campaigns can enrich your data pool.

Scrutinizing Audience Behavior: TikTok's Analytics Dashboard offers deep-dives into your target audience's demographics, interests, and behaviors. This treasure-trove of information can streamline your optimization efforts, enabling you to tailor your messages to resonate better with your audience.

Enhancing Ad Creatives: Iteratively refining your ad creatives can spur performance. Revise and polish your visuals, captions, or calls-to-action based on the insights you garner, and try various creative elements to discover what resonates most with your target audience.

Perfecting Audience Targeting: Streamline your ad reach and engagement by refining your targeting choices using the insights you've gleaned from your campaigns. Test different demographic groups, geographic regions, interests, or behaviors to unearth the most responsive audience segment.

Optimizing Budget Deployment: Strategic budget allocation, based on campaign performance, can enhance your ROI. Dedicate a larger share of your budget to the campaigns and targeting options that yield the best results and keep a close eye on the cost-per-result to optimize budget distribution.

Leveraging Lessons Learnt: Iterate and enhance your future campaigns using the insights gathered from current ones. Continually analyzing performance metrics, experimenting with fresh strategies, and staying updated with TikTok's latest trends and features can keep you ahead in the game.

Prioritizing Continuous Monitoring: Track your campaign performance over time to identify potential trends or spikes in engagement, conversion rates, or other key metrics. This data can inform your ad scheduling strategy, helping to maximize campaign effectiveness.

Optimizing Ad Placement: Pay heed to how your ads perform across various TikTok features - whether it's the main feed, the Discover section, or hashtag challenges. Adjust your bid and budget allocations based on these observations to augment your campaign's efficacy.

Regulating Ad Exposure: Be mindful of the exposure frequency of your ads. Excessive ad frequency may lead to viewer fatigue and decreased performance. If you observe a dip in engagement or conversion rates, consider adjusting the exposure cap to limit the frequency with which an individual user sees your ad.

Exploring Audience Segmentation: Harness audience segmentation features to target ads at specific user groups based on demographics, geographic locations, interests, or behaviors. This can help enhance engagement and conversion rates.These strategies can significantly improve your TikTok ad campaigns, enabling you to leverage your efforts for maximum effect. By focusing on optimization, you can ensure that every ad dollar spent delivers the best possible return on your investment.

CHAPTER 6

STRATEGIZING FOR TIKTOK: A COMPREHENSIVE GUIDE TO ADVERTISING STANDARDS

TikTok's ascendancy in the digital marketing world has placed a spotlight on its unique rules for advertisers. These guidelines and policies safeguard the platform's integrity, ensuring the user experience remains positive and secure. The following insights reveal TikTok's vital policies and their implications for marketers:

Content Specifications: Advertisements on TikTok must be fit for consumption by a diverse audience, devoid of explicit or offensive material. They must comply with ethical and legal standards and avoid promoting harmful activities, such as hate speech, drugs, or violence. Ads must be free of deceptive claims and maintain truth in advertising.

Restrictions on Specific Content: TikTok bars certain kinds of content from ads, including political advertisements, ads focusing on sensitive or divisive subjects, and promotions of illegal or counterfeit items. Marketers must craft their messages to be in line with TikTok's policies.

Copyright and Intellectual Property Rights: Advertisers are required to respect the copyright and intellectual property rights of others. They are forbidden from using copyrighted material without proper permission. All ad content should be original or properly licensed.

Emphasizing Safety and Privacy: The platform takes user safety and privacy very seriously. Therefore, advertisers must commit to user data protection and follow relevant privacy laws.

Openness and Disclosure: To maintain trust within the TikTok community, advertisers must promote transparency in their ads and provide explicit disclosures, ensuring that advertisements are easily identifiable as such.

Community Standards: TikTok's Community Guidelines apply to all content, whether paid or organic. All advertisers must ensure that their content respects these rules, maintaining the platform's standards for respect and inclusivity.

Audience Targeting: Advertisers must respect TikTok's regulations for audience targeting, including strict adherence to age restrictions and privacy concerns, especially for users below 13 years old.

Ad Evaluation: TikTok examines all advertisements before publication to ensure they align with the platform's rules. Marketers should account for this review period when planning their campaigns.

Creative Parameters: TikTok has specific requirements for ad creatives such as video format, aspect ratio, file size, and duration. Marketers should comply with these to ensure smooth playback and an optimal user experience.

Brand Protection: TikTok values brand safety. Advertisers should take measures to avoid their ads from appearing alongside inappropriate or offensive content.

Call-to-Action (CTA): Including a clear and engaging CTA in advertisements is advised to spur user engagement.

Compliance with Local Regulations: Advertisers must ensure their ads align with all local laws and regulations, including advertising standards and data protection laws.

Authenticity and Transparency: TikTok encourages advertisers to be open and genuine in their content. Ads that feature real experiences, user-generated content, or product demonstrations tend to resonate with the TikTok community.

Ongoing Compliance: Regular reviewing and optimizing of ad content, addressing user feedback, and promptly dealing with violations or issues are crucial.

Disclosure of Partnerships: In collaborations with influencers or third parties for sponsored content, disclosing partnerships transparently is necessary to maintain trust within the community.

Finally, it is incumbent upon the advertiser to ensure their ads adhere to TikTok's guidelines. Being familiar with the rules and staying updated on changes will prevent any violations and ensure a successful advertising campaign on this rapidly evolving platform.

CHAPTER 7

FUTURE SCENARIOS AND TRANSFORMATIVE DEVELOPMENTS

E-commerce Symbiosis As TikTok steers towards becoming an all-inclusive ecosystem, it is weaving e-commerce into its tapestry. Signs like embedded in-app purchase options and ad-associated product page links point towards a sea change. This commitment to enriching user experience translates into a goldmine for marketers, offering a direct route to conversions and sales in the times ahead.

The Age of Augmented Reality Augmented Reality (AR) is not just a trend on TikTok; it's a revolution. From creators to businesses, everyone's leveraging AR filters and effects. TikTok's exploration of AR advertising opens doors to more immersive, interactive campaigns. With AR, brands get to break the mold, engaging users and strengthening brand loyalty in unprecedented ways.

Personalization: The Winning Approach TikTok understands the currency of relevance. It's upping the ante on personalization to serve more engaging, pertinent content. Marketers, armed with advanced targeting and customization tools, can craft ads finely tuned to user preferences, behaviors, and interests, leading to improved engagement and effectiveness.

The New Age of Influencer Marketing Influencer marketing isn't static; it's evolving on TikTok. The future holds sophisticated collaborations, long-term partnerships, and brand ambassador programs. With new features and tools to support these partnerships, advertisers can assess their campaigns' impact more accurately and plan better.

Community-focused, Vertical Content As TikTok grows, it's catering to an array of interests and niches. Advertisers can seize this opportunity by crafting content specific to certain niches. By appealing to distinct communities and interests, brands can connect with relevant audiences, enhancing conversions and engagement.

User-Generated Content: The Secret Sauce UGC on TikTok is more than a trend; it's a mainstay. Encouraging users to create brand-related content, advertisers can build authenticity and loyalty. Incorporating UGC into campaigns boosts user engagement, raises brand awareness, and fosters a sense of community.

Decoding Insights for Better Decisions TikTok's future includes comprehensive analytics and insights. Advertisers can leverage these data-driven insights to fine-tune their campaigns, refine targeting strategies, and elevate overall performance.

The Cross-Platform Boom As TikTok's popularity swells, advertisers can anticipate expanded opportunities for cross-platform advertising and integration. This paves the way for comprehensive advertising strategies across various platforms, reaching a larger audience.

Video Rules the Roost Video is the heart and soul of TikTok and remains the most potent advertising format. Creating compelling, snackable videos that align with TikTok's vibrant spirit should be a priority for advertisers.

The Global Odyssey TikTok's influence transcends borders, making global expansion inevitable. Advertisers can tap into this international growth by tailoring campaigns to diverse cultures and regions.

Brand Alliances and Collaborations Brand partnerships with TikTok influencers are skyrocketing. Advertisers can expect more collaboration opportunities, co-created content, and partnerships, enhancing brand visibility within the TikTok community.

Live Streaming: The Real-time Connection Live streaming is fast gaining momentum on TikTok, enabling real-time audience interactions.

Brands can use this feature for interactive experiences like product launches, Q&A sessions, and exclusive behind-the-scenes content.

Authenticity is the New Currency TikTok thrives on authenticity and user-centric content. Brands should aim to create content that chimes with TikTok's user base, encourages participation, and embraces trending topics.

Influencer Amplification Influencer-created content, when repurposed or incorporated into campaigns, has the potential to amplify a brand's reach and resonate with audiences. This method combines the authenticity of influencers with the extensive reach of the platform.

CHAPTER 8

INITIATING THE TIKTOK MARKETING JOURNEY

Entering the bustling world of TikTok as an advertiser necessitates a sequential setup. Let's traverse through the process:

Crafting Your Advertiser Profile: Kick-start your journey at the TikTok Ads Manager portal. Click on "Create an Ads Account", and sign up using your professional email or an existing social media account.

Furnishing Business Information: Provide relevant details about your business, like name, website, industry, and contact info. Be meticulous and ensure the data is current and precise.

Profile Verification: TikTok might request account verification to establish your business legitimacy. This might involve the submission of additional documentation, such as business licenses or ID proofs.

Launching Campaigns: After your profile setup and verification, dive into your inaugural ad campaign. Define your campaign goals like boosting website traffic, escalating app installs, or garnering video views. Set an appropriate budget to accompany these objectives.

Fine-Tuning Ad Preferences: Pinpoint your target demographic based on factors like location, age, gender, interests, etc. TikTok provides a host of targeting features, enabling you to reach distinct user segments. Additionally, determine ad placement preferences and ad formats that dovetail with your campaign objectives.

Creative Strategy: Design compelling ad creatives adhering to TikTok's best practices and guidelines. This usually involves crafting short-form videos that snatch attention and efficiently deliver your message. Utilize TikTok's in-app video creation tools or upload your own videos.

Performance Tracking: Incorporate ad tracking measures for accurate campaign performance evaluation. TikTok offers tracking pixels and third-party tracking tool integration to monitor vital metrics like impressions, clicks, conversions, etc.

Pre-launch Evaluation: Inspect all the details and settings to ensure they match your objectives before launching your campaign. Upon satisfaction, submit your campaign for review by TikTok's ad moderation team, which ensures your ad content aligns with their policies and guidelines.

Payment Setup: To roll out ads on TikTok, establish your payment method. TikTok accepts various payment modes, including credit cards and PayPal. Fill in your payment details and ensure you have enough funds to cover your ad expenditure.

Ad Scheduling: Decide your ad schedule and delivery. Opt for specific start and end dates or a continuous campaign. Also, determine ad delivery preferences, such as standard or accelerated delivery, according to your campaign goals and budget.

Ad Placement Strategy: TikTok provides varied ad placement options, including in-feed ads, brand takeovers, top view ads, etc. Depending on your campaign objectives, pick an ad placement that complements your goals and target audience.

Conversion Tracking Setup: If tracking conversions is your campaign objective, set up the necessary conversion tracking. This could involve integrating TikTok's conversion tracking pixel on your website or using third-party tracking tools.

Ongoing Campaign Monitoring: Post-campaign launch, keep a close eye on its performance. Scrutinize key metrics like impressions, clicks, click-through rates, and conversions to assess your ads' effectiveness. Make necessary adjustments to improve performance and achieve your campaign objectives.

Scaling and Iterating: Gain insights from your ad campaigns and consider scaling your successful campaigns by boosting your budget, expanding your target audience, or experimenting with new ad formats. Continually refine your advertising strategy based on data-driven insights to maximize your return on investment (ROI).

Support and Resources: TikTok offers extensive support resources, such as tutorials, guides, and a dedicated support team to aid advertisers. Make the most of these resources to deepen your understanding of TikTok advertising best practices and to address any issues you may encounter.

CHAPTER 9

NAVIGATING THE COMPLEXITIES OF TIKTOK'S ADVERTISING LANDSCAPE

In the intricate landscape of TikTok advertising, the ad allocation and bidding mechanism form the core foundation. Every time a user immerses into the platform, TikTok skillfully scrutinizes potential ad spaces, considering aspects like user behaviors, inclinations, and demographic specifics.

The tale then unfolds from the perspective of the advertiser. The selection of the target audience, investment boundaries, and the distinct creative aspects present in the ad, significantly influence the ad's trajectory. At this juncture, the concept of a Relevance Index comes into play. This index assigns a score to each ad based on elements like ad quality, user interaction, and historical success records. This score is a crucial determiner of the ad's likelihood of securing a placement.

Next, the concept of Ad Priority steps into the limelight. Influenced by its relevance score, the bid value, and other factors, this priority decides the sequence in which the ads are displayed to the users.

Ads with a superior priority score are then selected for display, finding their place in various locations within the platform, from the user's feed to other specialized sections.

When it comes to managing bids, TikTok offers the choice of manual or automated bidding. Manual bidding empowers advertisers with the control of determining bid amounts, while the automated option assigns this task to TikTok, allowing it to adjust the bids to match the campaign's goals and budget. Here, advertisers also establish a cap on the amount they're willing to pay to accomplish their campaign objectives, which can range from generating impressions and clicks to driving conversions.

Furthermore, advertisers designate either a daily or lifetime budget for their campaign, an amount that should mirror the advertiser's goals, the intended scope, and frequency of the ad campaign. Unlike traditional systems, TikTok's ad placement process is a dynamic, real-time affair. Every user interaction sets off a fresh evaluation of bids and ad positions.

The cost for each ad view is guided by the second-highest bid in the placement round.

However, advertisers only part with their bid amount if their ad is victorious in securing a slot. The position of the ad, in turn, influences its visibility to users.

Throughout the campaign, advertisers are free to keep track of their ad's performance, tweaking their bids and strategies as required. This continual process of optimization, driven by data insights, can lead to significant improvements in ad effectiveness and return on investment.

While the bidding process can vary based on the specifics of the ad format, campaign goals, and the selected audience, TikTok does provide further direction on bid placement and campaign performance enhancement. Gaining a deep understanding of this complex ad placement process and effectively managing it can lead to a substantial increase in the effectiveness of an advertiser's campaigns, helping them fulfill their marketing objectives on TikTok.

CHAPTER 10

NAVIGATING THE TIKTOK AD LANDSCAPE: COMPREHENSIVE POLICIES AND GUIDELINES

Engaging with the vibrant TikTok community necessitates adherence to an array of carefully crafted advertising policies and guidelines. This chapter unravels the specifics of this framework and elucidates key principles advertisers should respect to preserve the platform's integrity and safeguard the user experience.

A key cornerstone of TikTok's ad policy is the prohibition of certain content categories. To safeguard the platform's wholesome ambiance, advertising illegal activities, harmful substances, counterfeit goods, and adult content is strictly off-limits. Deceptive practices are similarly shunned. Advertisers should strive for truthful representation in their campaigns, ensuring the authenticity and accuracy of their ads to preserve user trust.

Maintaining the community's tranquility extends to respecting the rules against harassment, hate speech, violence, or other disruptive behavior. Advertisers, too, fall within the purview of TikTok's Community Guidelines.

Intellectual property rights further underpin the platform's policies, emphasizing respect for copyrights, trademarks, and other proprietary rights, underscoring that unauthorized use of such materials is unacceptable.

TikTok also provides detailed guidance for each ad format. Advertisers should acquaint themselves with these specifics related to in-feed ads, branded effects, and hashtag challenges, ensuring their campaigns meet TikTok's technical and creative standards. In the same vein, TikTok establishes constraints on sensitive content and dictates respectful and appropriate engagement with sensitive events or social issues in ads.

Underlying these guidelines is a stern commitment to data privacy, requiring advertisers to comply with all applicable laws. This encompasses the acquisition of proper user consent for data collection, storage, and processing, with the necessity to transparently communicate data practices to users.

Targeting restrictions are also enforced to protect certain user categories. For example, particular care should be exercised when aiming ads at children or specific age groups.

Moreover, advertisers must be aware of the platform's ad review process, allowing ample time for their ads to be evaluated for compliance with TikTok's stringent standards.

Given the dynamic nature of the platform, advertisers must adopt an ongoing compliance approach, consistently updating their ads and remaining informed about policy modifications. An emphasis is placed on transparent advertising, requiring clear disclosure of any paid partnerships or promotions. This stems from TikTok's commitment to brand safety and avoidance of harmful content association.

When navigating political and social issues, compliance with guidelines, local regulations, and necessary disclaimers is paramount. Ads targeted at minors must respect their privacy and comply with age restrictions. The same adherence to local laws and industry standards is required when targeting ads in specific regions.

Collaborations with influencers necessitate that their content aligns with TikTok's policies. Clear instructions regarding ad disclosures and content requirements must be communicated to influencers.

TikTok also encourages user feedback on ads, rigorously enforcing its policies via automated systems and human review.

Failure to adhere to TikTok's policies carries significant consequences, from ad rejection to account suspension, or even legal actions in severe cases. To avoid these pitfalls, advertisers are advised to thoroughly familiarize themselves with TikTok's comprehensive advertising policies and guidelines. Abiding by these guidelines guarantees a smooth advertising experience, ensuring the preservation of the vibrant and engaging TikTok community.

CHAPTER 11

STRATEGIC INSIGHTS INTO CRAFTING TIKTOK ADS

In the constantly evolving realm of TikTok advertising, sticking to innovative strategies helps ensure the effectiveness of your campaign. This chapter offers tips and tactics to boost your reach and impact on the platform.

Tapping Into the Pulse of TikTok: TikTok is characterized by its dynamic, unique style. It's essential to engage with the platform's culture, trends, and creative formats to forge connections with its users. Through humor, authenticity, and creative expression, your ads can echo the TikTok vibe and hold attention.

Brevity is Key: On TikTok, short, crisp content rules the roost. Prioritize capturing attention within the initial seconds and convey your message promptly. Videos of 15 to 30 seconds duration tend to retain viewer engagement.

Storytelling Through Visuals: Leverage visuals to weave a compelling narrative that resonates with your target audience. Utilize vibrant hues, captivating graphics, and innovative transitions to draw viewers in. Maintain an energetic visual tempo to retain interest.

Explicit Brand Visibility: Make sure your brand takes center stage in your ad. Incorporate your logo, brand colors, and other visual elements aligned with your brand identity. Consistency in branding across ads can bolster brand recognition and association.

Harnessing User-Generated Content: TikTok thrives on content created by its users. By incorporating such content in your ads, you can lend them a touch of authenticity and relatability. Inspire users to participate in challenges or share their brand experiences.

Persuasive Call-to-Action (CTA): Each ad should have a clear, compelling CTA guiding viewers towards their next step. Whether it's website visits, app downloads, or purchases, clearly articulate your desired action. A visually appealing and easily comprehensible CTA can be very effective.

Trial and Refinement: Conduct experiments with diverse ad variations to ascertain what best resonates with your target audience. Testing different visuals, messages, music, and formats can help optimize ad performance. Analyze the obtained data and refine your creative strategy based on these insights.

Trend Adaptation: Keep your finger on the pulse of the latest TikTok trends and challenges. By integrating these trends into your ad, you tap into the platform's viral nature, thereby boosting your ad's chances of being shared and engaged with.

Respecting Your Audience: Cultivate a respectful, inclusive approach in your ad content. Avoid offensive language, stereotypes, or controversial themes. Create content that celebrates diversity, promotes positivity, and aligns with the values of the TikTok community.

Engage Users Early: Hook your viewers in the initial seconds of your ad. An intriguing opening scene or a curious question can stimulate viewer interest and encourage continued watching.

User Engagement: Leverage the platform's interactive features to engage users. Invite users to like, comment, share, or participate in challenges related to your ad.

The more participatory your ad, the greater the chances of user engagement and sharing.

Influencer Partnerships: Collaborate with popular TikTok influencers who share your brand ethos and target audience.

Influencers can create engaging content that resonates with their followers, thereby boosting engagement and brand exposure.

Harnessing Humor: Humor is a potent tool on TikTok. Incorporate it into your ads to make them entertaining and shareable. Use TikTok trends, memes, or viral jokes to add a fun twist to your content.

Visual Effects and Filters: Experiment with TikTok's array of visual effects, filters, and augmented reality (AR) features. Use effects that enhance your message or align with your brand's aesthetic.

Ad Format Testing: TikTok offers several ad formats like in-feed ads, brand takeovers, and branded effects. Experiment with these formats to determine what resonates best with your target audience and aligns with your campaign goals.

Localization: Customize your ads to resonate with specific regional audiences.

Tailor the content, language, or cultural references for a more personalized viewer experience across different markets.

Cross-Promotion: Use your TikTok ads to drive traffic to your other social media channels or website.

Encourage viewers to follow your TikTok account, visit your website, or engage with your content across different platforms.

CHAPTER 12

DECODING AND LEVERAGING TIKTOK AD ANALYTICS

In the world of TikTok advertising, your ad campaigns' success hinges on your understanding and optimization of analytics. TikTok offers a multitude of analytical tools and tracking resources designed to give advertisers the necessary insights to refine their campaign strategies. Here's a fresh perspective on how to navigate and utilize the sea of data at your disposal:

TikTok Pixel: An invaluable tool, the TikTok Pixel lets you observe user activities on your website post-TikTok ad interaction. It offers insights into conversions, facilitates campaign fine-tuning, and aids in creating custom audiences for retargeting purposes.

Analytics Dashboard - TikTok Ads Manager: This comprehensive platform presents critical metrics such as impressions, clicks, conversions, and engagement rates. Moreover, it gives a detailed breakdown of data based on ad formats, sets, and targeting options.

Performance Indicators: TikTok serves an array of metrics including views, CTR, CPA, ROAS, conversion rates, and engagement rates. By analyzing these metrics, you can pinpoint areas of improvement and make data-informed decisions.

Audience Insights: TikTok's audience insights offer valuable demographic data about the users interacting with your ads, providing you with the knowledge to hone your targeting strategies.

A/B Testing: The TikTok Ads Manager facilitates comparison tests between different ad variations, allowing you to identify the highest performing ads and optimize your campaigns accordingly.

Detailed Campaign Reports: These reports give a comprehensive overview of your campaign's performance, tracking trends over time, and highlighting areas requiring adjustments.

Customizable Data Views: TikTok's analytics tools offer customization of data views and report exporting, enabling external data analysis and easy sharing with stakeholders.

Conversion Tracking: This feature enables tracking of specific user actions post ad click, thus illuminating the effectiveness of your campaigns.

Attribution Models: TikTok provides diverse attribution models to understand the user journey and credit conversions to specific ad interactions.

Real-Time Monitoring: This function lets you keep a close eye on your campaign's performance, enabling prompt adjustments and effective budget allocation.

Audience Segmentation: TikTok analytics enables audience segmentation based on demographics, interests, and more, facilitating a better understanding of audience response to your ads.

Benchmarking: Compare your campaign performance against industry benchmarks to identify areas for improvement.

Content Strategy Insights: The performance data can provide valuable information on the type of content that resonates best with your audience, shaping your content strategy.

Cross-Platform Analysis: This allows for performance comparison across platforms, helping you understand the overall impact of your advertising efforts.

Experimentation and Iteration: Continually experiment with different creatives, messaging, targeting options, and bidding strategies to optimize your ad campaigns based on the insights garnered from tracking and analytics.

Navigating the intricate world of TikTok ad analytics doesn't have to be intimidating. By understanding and leveraging the vast array of tools and insights available, you can ensure your ad campaigns are data-driven, optimized, and successful.

CHAPTER 13

FOCUSING YOUR AIM – AUDIENCE SPECIALIZATION

Identifying and effectively reaching out to your intended audience is a fundamental piece of the puzzle when it comes to successful TikTok ad campaigns. The following points provide guidance on how to focus your aim and successfully specialize your audience on TikTok:

Segmenting by Demographics: TikTok enables you to filter your ad reach based on a range of demographic indicators such as age, gender, and geographic location. Appropriately aligning these options with your audience demographics is critical for ensuring your ads find their way to the right viewers.

Tailoring to Interests: The platform also affords you the luxury of targeting individuals who display an interest in specific fields or activities. This enables you to select related interest categories that sync with your offering and effectively narrow down your audience.

Creating Custom Audiences: TikTok offers the facility to develop custom audiences derived from your existing customer data. It's possible to use existing customer lists or app event data to pinpoint precise customer segments or to reconnect with previous customers.

Expanding with Lookalike Audiences: TikTok's lookalike audiences feature is a powerful tool that allows you to broaden your reach to users who bear resemblance to your existing customers or website visitors.

Using this tool, you can aim your ads at individuals sharing characteristics and habits similar to your perfect audience.

Leveraging Behavior: TikTok also affords behavioral targeting options which consider user engagement patterns on the platform. By targeting users who interact with specific content, respond to certain ads, or display behaviors in line with your campaign objectives, you can enhance the effectiveness of your campaigns.

Retargeting and Remarketing: TikTok offers tools that allow you to retarget users who have previously interacted with your ads or visited your website. These features allow you to reintroduce your brand, products, or services, and inspire users to undertake desired actions.

Device and Connectivity: The TikTok platform also allows you to target ads based on the type of device a user operates and their type of internet connection. Such options are beneficial for ads optimization, taking into consideration device capabilities and connection speed.

Excluding Audiences: TikTok's exclusion targeting feature allows you to deliberately keep certain audience segments or categories from viewing your ads, helping to ensure that your content is seen by the most relevant viewers.

Audience Specialization: Once you've established your target audience, consider breaking it down further based on precise criteria such as lifecycle stage, purchase habits, or engagement levels. By specializing your audience, you can customize your ads and creative content to better suit specific segments, thereby boosting ad relevance and efficacy.

Experimentation and Refinement: It's essential to persistently experiment and refine your targeting strategies. Try out different targeting combinations and audience segments to pinpoint the most effective strategy for your campaign goals.

Regularly analyze performance data and make data-driven modifications to boost targeting accuracy and enhance your results.

Geotargeting: TikTok also provides the ability to target users based on their geographic location, ideal for local or regional businesses that want to reach users in specific areas.

Linguistic Reach: TikTok also provides language targeting options, allowing you to reach users who communicate in particular languages.

Behavioral Targeting: TikTok extends its behavioral targeting options beyond basic demographics. By targeting users based on their past behavior on TikTok, you can reach users who are likely to be interested in your products or services.

TikTok Creator Partnership: The TikTok Creator Marketplace provides an avenue for advertisers to connect with content creators who align with their target audience, enabling them to reach and engage their ideal demographic.

Multi-Dimensional Targeting: TikTok allows you to amalgamate various targeting options to build a more refined and accurate audience segment. By employing multi-dimensional targeting, you can reach an extremely specific group of users who are more likely to be interested in your ads.

Trying Out Different Segments: Do not hesitate to test out different audience segments and targeting options. A/B testing can assist you in comparing the performance of different segments and targeting strategies, helping you identify the most effective combination for your campaigns.

In a nutshell, understanding the diverse targeting and segmentation strategies that TikTok offers can play a pivotal role in steering your ad campaigns towards success.

CHAPTER 14

ENHANCING YOUR TIKTOK AD CAMPAIGNS: STRATEGIES FOR OPTIMIZATION

The secret to supercharging your TikTok ad campaigns lies in an all-important process: optimization. By fine-tuning your strategies, you can maximize the results of your ad campaigns. Here's a guide to the most effective techniques:

1. The Foundation: Set Clear Goals Commence with clearly articulating your campaign objectives. Whether you're aiming to generate website traffic, increase brand visibility, garner leads, or augment sales, having precise goals sets the stage for directed optimization and success evaluation.

2. Stay on Track: Monitor and Analyze Regularly Make use of the analytics tools at your disposal to scrutinize your ad campaign's performance continuously. Keep track of critical parameters such as impressions, click-through rates (CTR), engagement rates, conversions, and return on ad spend (ROAS). Study this data to unearth trends and areas for enhancement.

3. Trial and Error: Employ A/B Testing Introduce A/B testing to compare distinct elements of your ads and discover what appeals most to your target audience. Examine various aspects of your creative, ad copy, call-to-action, landing pages, and even different targeting options. This method allows you to refine your ads with insights driven by data.

4. The Art of the Ad: Fine-Tuning the Creative Aspect Invest time in honing your ad creatives. Try

various visuals, messaging techniques, storytelling styles, and ad formats to determine the most persuasive combination. Keep your content fresh and engaging to hold user attention and boost campaign results.

5. The Power of Words: Perfecting Ad Copy Don't underestimate the importance of a well-crafted ad copy. Ensure it is lucid, succinct, and alluring. Use attention-grabbing headlines, compelling call-to-actions, and emphasize the value of your offering. Experiment with different versions to identify what elicits the best audience response.

6. Know Your Audience: Refining Targeting Strategies Regularly evaluate your targeting strategies. Your performance data will reveal which audience segments are reacting positively to your ads. Adjust your parameters like demographics, interests, and behaviors to concentrate on the most relevant segments.

7. Optimal Bidding: Enhancing Bid Strategies Revise your bidding strategy for maximum ad spend value. Try different bid types, like cost-per-click (CPC) or cost-per-thousand impressions (CPM), and vary your bid amounts based on ad performance. Stay competitive in the auction by continually adjusting your bids.

8. Full Circle: Conversion Optimization If conversions are your campaign goal, prioritize optimization of your landing pages, checkout processes, and user flows. The user experience must be seamless, with optimized load times and intuitive conversion process.

9. Keeping It Fresh: Managing Ad Fatigue Maintaining an ideal ad frequency helps prevent ad fatigue. Overexposing your audience to the same ads can yield diminishing returns. Hence, rotate your ads, refresh your creative content, and tweak your targeting.

10. Stay Agile: Embrace the Iterative Approach Optimization is an ongoing journey. Constantly revisit your campaign performance, gather insights, and refine your strategies. Be responsive to shifts in user behavior, market trends, and platform updates.

11. Seek Expert Advice: Collaborate with TikTok Support Should you encounter optimization issues or have queries, TikTok's advertiser support team is there to assist. They can provide guidance specific to your campaign objectives.

12. Time It Right: Ad Scheduling The timing of your ads can significantly affect engagement. Identify peak periods and schedule your ads accordingly, considering user behavior patterns, time zones, and specific days of high activity.

13. Position Matters: Ad Placement Optimization TikTok offers a variety of ad placements. Test different ones to identify which deliver the best results for your campaign goals.

14. Find the Balance: Ad Duration and Frequency Experiment with different ad durations and frequencies. Adjust the balance between reach and user engagement to find what works best.

15. Rekindle the Connection: Retargeting and Remarketing Use retargeting and remarketing strategies to reengage users who have previously interacted with your ads or website. Tailoring your messaging to this audience could increase conversions due to prior engagement with your brand.

CHAPTER 15

SYNERGISTIC ADVERTISING AND INTEGRATED CHANNEL MARKETING

Harnessing the power of synergistic advertising and integrated channel marketing can play a pivotal role in broadening your audience spectrum, enhancing brand recognition, and multiplying the efficacy of your TikTok promotional endeavors. Let's delve deeper into these strategies:

Synergistic Advertising - Social Media Outlets: Leverage your established digital presence across platforms such as Instagram, Facebook, Twitter, and YouTube to heighten the awareness of your TikTok promotions. Distribute short clips or notable moments from your TikTok content on these platforms, redirecting users to your TikTok account or specific clips. This approach can result in increased traffic flow, boosted engagement, and acquisition of new followers.

Web Synergy: Incorporate TikTok content into your website via embedded videos or unique sections dedicated to flaunt your TikTok activity. This tactic not only familiarizes website visitors with your TikTok content but also amplifies brand visibility and fuels cross-platform interaction.

Email Outreach: Utilize your email marketing endeavors to push your TikTok content and ads. Embed videos or include hyperlinks in your email newsletters or specialized campaigns to inspire subscribers to follow your TikTok profile and interact with your content.

Influencer Synergy: Engage with influencers across various platforms for a mutual promotion of your TikTok content. Team up with influencers with a substantial TikTok following as well as a prominent social media presence. They can produce content showcasing your TikTok promotions, share it with their followers, and generate traffic for your TikTok account or videos.

Integrated Channel Marketing - Display Advertisements: Execute display ads on other websites or mobile applications to divert traffic to your TikTok profile. Display ads can amplify brand awareness and attract users who might not be TikTok active but are engaged on other digital platforms.

YouTube Ad Integration: YouTube, being a popular hub for video content, can supplement your TikTok promotional efforts. Develop YouTube advertisements that highlight your TikTok content or boost your TikTok profile, motivating YouTube users to interact with your TikTok content.

Native Ad Integration: Experiment with native advertising on relevant platforms or media channels. Native ads are designed to blend into the platform's content, offering a non-intrusive ad experience. Feature your TikTok content in these ads or incorporate links to your profile, inviting users to engage with your TikTok presence.

Influencer Synergy on Alternative Platforms: Collaborate with influencers on platforms such as Instagram, YouTube, or Twitch who can endorse your TikTok content or run sponsored posts featuring your ads.

This can help introduce their existing audience to your TikTok presence, promoting cross-channel engagement and extending your reach.

Traditional Marketing Strategies: Consider integrating your TikTok information into your offline marketing materials like print ads, billboards, or TV commercials. Include your TikTok handle or QR codes to prompt offline audiences to seek out and engage with your TikTok content.

Brand Alliances and Joint Ventures: Seek partnerships with brands or organizations that share your target demographic. Collaborate on joint campaigns, events, or initiatives involving mutual promotion on multiple channels. By leveraging each other's audiences, you can tap into new user bases and enhance brand visibility.

Maintaining brand consistency across diverse channels is crucial. Adjust your content and design elements to cater to the specific needs and preferences of each platform's audience while preserving a unified brand identity. By intertwining synergistic advertising and integrated channel marketing, you can supercharge the influence of your TikTok promotional campaigns, engage a broader audience, drive engagement, and achieve your marketing aspirations.

CHAPTER 16

STRATEGIZING PARTNERSHIPS

Exploiting the potency of collaborations with top TikTok content creators could boost your brand, products, or services. Here are some tips to make the most of these partnerships:

Spotting the Right Powerhouses Aim for content creators whose outputs sync with your brand's ethos, the demographics of your audience, and your campaign goals. Their audience demographics, quality of content, follower count, and engagement rate should inform your choice. Using TikTok's built-in search, influencer marketing tools, or liaising with influencer marketing agencies can help you find the right fit.

Understanding the Powerhouses Devote time to delve into the world of the influencers. Scrutinize their content, engagement statistics, past brand collaborations, and audience demographics to ascertain their suitability for your campaign. You should opt for influencers who have a genuine rapport with their followers and align with your brand's story.

Creating a Clear Roadmap Articulate your campaign goals clearly and make sure the influencers comprehend them. Whether it's spreading the word, spurring engagement, or highlighting a particular product, influencers should align their content to these goals.

Cultivating Genuine Bonds Reach out to influencers with a real appreciation of their work and a keen understanding of their audience's needs. Personalize your outreach, and highlight why you see them as an excellent fit for your brand. Genuine connections with influencers could lead to more impactful and successful partnerships.

Providing a Detailed Blueprint Offer a comprehensive campaign blueprint that includes essential messaging, content guidelines, any specific deliverables, and campaign requirements. Make sure they understand the desired stylistic and creative aspects you want them to infuse into their content. But remember to allow room for their creativity to ensure their content resonates with their audience while staying within campaign boundaries.

Discussing Compensation and Agreements Negotiate compensation based on aspects like their reach, engagement levels, and the amount of work involved. This could range from a flat fee, product samples, affiliate partnerships, or a mix. Contracts outlining collaboration terms, including deliverables, timelines, exclusivity clauses, and usage rights, are vital.

Working on Content Together Collaborate closely during content creation, providing feedback and guidance to ensure alignment with your brand story and resonance with your target audience. It's crucial to respect the influencers' creativity and their knack for crafting content that their followers can relate to.

Maintaining Compliance Ensure influencers adhere to the Federal Trade Commission's (FTC) guidelines for influencer marketing. Clearly labeled disclosures like #ad or #sponsored must be included in the content to indicate paid partnerships. Ensure influencers are familiar with and follow necessary guidelines.

Assessing Outcomes Monitor the results of influencer partnerships using TikTok's analytics tools and other measurement methods. Evaluate the collaborations' success based on metrics like reach, engagement, follower growth, website traffic, or conversions.

Use this information to fine-tune your future influencer strategies and optimize your campaigns.

Building Lasting Partnerships Think about forging long-lasting relationships with influencers whose work consistently aligns with your brand values and generates positive results. These ongoing partnerships can strengthen your connection with their audience and promote long-term brand recognition and loyalty.

Leveraging Content Across Platforms Encourage influencers to repurpose their TikTok content on other social media platforms. This strategy helps broaden the reach of their content beyond TikTok, touching different audience groups. For example, sharing teasers or highlights of their TikTok videos on Instagram, YouTube, or Twitter could direct followers to their TikTok profile or the full video.

Running Contests and Giveaways Collaborate with influencers to run contests or giveaways on TikTok to create a buzz, increase engagement, and gain new followers. Influencers can craft content that showcases the giveaway or contest, demonstrating the prizes and prompting their followers to participate by following your TikTok account, liking the video, or leaving comments.

Telling a Story Work with influencers to weave compelling narratives that incorporate your brand subtly.

Rather than overt promotional content, focus on integrating your brand into engaging stories or challenges that resonate with the influencer's audience.

This method results in a more natural and organic integration of your brand message.

Holding Live Streams and Q&A Sessions Collaborate with influencers for live streams and Q&A sessions, providing a real-time connection between your brand and their audience.
This direct interaction can deepen the audience's engagement with your brand and provide valuable feedback.

CHAPTER 17

FINANCIAL STRATEGIES AND EXPENDITURE PLANNING

When it comes to formulating your financial strategy and expenditure planning for advertising on TikTok, it's vital to recognize various aspects that may influence your overall investment. Let's explore some critical factors to bear in mind:

Diversity of Ad Models: Various ad models on TikTok could potentially have different pricing tiers. For instance, in-feed ads, sponsored filters, and hashtag campaigns might carry different cost parameters. Align your budget with the ad types that best suit your marketing objectives.

Audience Segmentation: TikTok facilitates multiple audience segmentation methods to reach specific demographics, interests, or behavioral patterns. The pricing of your ads could fluctuate based on the audience segment chosen. Narrow or specialized segmentation could be costlier compared to a generalized audience.

Bidding Methodology: TikTok employs a bidding system, allowing advertisers to bid for ad placements competitively. Establish your bidding method based on your marketing aims and budget. You can opt for either automatic bidding, with TikTok optimizing the bids based on your goals, or manual bidding, where you set the desired bid amount.

Campaign Timeline: The timeline of your TikTok ad campaign can significantly influence your overall budget.
Extensive campaigns might necessitate larger budget allocations, whereas condensed campaigns could permit more precise spending within a set timeframe.

Collaborations with Influencers: Should you decide to partner with TikTok influencers, bear in mind that their fees can vary extensively based on their follower count, engagement rate, and influence level. You'll need to negotiate remuneration and account for additional costs like content creation, exclusivity, or product gifting.

Creative Development: Crafting high-caliber and captivating ad content might involve expenses like video production, editing, graphic design, and music licensing. Structure your creative development budget to ensure your ads are visually compelling and resonate with your target audience.

Experimental Adjustments: Dedicate a portion of your budget for experimental adjustments. It's crucial to observe your ads' performance, fine-tune creative elements, tweak audience parameters, and refine your campaigns based on data insights. Testing various strategies can enhance campaign performance and cost efficiency.

Service Charges and Minimum Expenditure: TikTok might have service charges or minimum expenditure prerequisites depending on your advertising objectives, target market, or campaign size. Ensure you comprehend the platform's pricing structure and guidelines to understand the cost implications.

Periodic Demand Variations: Factor in periodic demand changes and peak periods that could affect advertising costs. For instance, holiday seasons or major events might intensify demand and raise ad costs due to heightened competition. Structure your budget accordingly and modify bidding strategies to optimize results during these periods.

ROI Evaluation: Establish key performance indicators (KPIs) and metrics to measure your TikTok ad campaigns' return on investment (ROI) as you apportion your budget. Tracking conversions, engagement, and other pertinent metrics will guide you in assessing your spending's effectiveness and making informed decisions for future budget allocations.

Remember, the success of your TikTok marketing campaign hinges on carefully considering these elements and making data-driven decisions. The cost of marketing on TikTok is flexible, making it a suitable choice for brands of all sizes and budgets.

CHAPTER 18

ACING THE GLOBAL STAGE WITH TIKTOK MARKETING

Gaining worldwide traction on TikTok can be a compelling method to capture a diverse, international audience and elevate your brand's prominence across distinct markets. Here are some factors to consider when executing global marketing campaigns on TikTok:

In-Depth Market Assessment: Conduct comprehensive market analysis to pinpoint areas where TikTok has a significant user concentration and your potential audience resides. Grasp cultural subtleties, user tendencies, and predilections in each market to customize your promotional tactics.

Customization for Local Markets: Frame your promotional content in a way that strikes a chord with audiences in different regions. Make sure your ads, captions, and call-to-action statements are translated to the local language for better understanding and interaction. Adapt your creative components, like visuals and music, to match each market's cultural context.

Focused Geographic Marketing: Utilize TikTok's targeting options to concentrate your promotional efforts on distinct regions or countries. Geographical targeting ensures your content reaches users in the intended locations. Fine-tune your targeting strategies based on demographics, interests, or behaviors relevant to each market.

Ad Trends and Types: Stay updated with trending ad formats in each market.

Ad types on TikTok, like in-feed ads, branded effects, or sponsored hashtag challenges, might vary in popularity across regions. Modify your creative strategies to align with the preferences of the local TikTok community.

Collaborations with Local Influencers: Partner with influencers from each target market to augment your brand's outreach and authenticity. These collaborations can boost your connection with the local audience and drive engagement. Ensure your chosen influencers are authentic and resonate with your brand ethos.

Cultural Considerations: Acknowledge cultural sensitivities and societal norms when planning your ad campaigns. Avoid material that could potentially offend or be deemed inappropriate in certain markets.

Compliance with Local Guidelines: Become conversant with the specific advertising regulations and guidelines in each targeted country or region. Comply with the respective legal and regulatory requirements in each market.

Currency and Pricing Strategy: Account for currency exchange rates and pricing disparities in each market. Allocate your budget based on factors like market size, competition, and purchasing power. Modify your bidding strategies and budget pacing to optimize your expenditure.

Performance Analysis and Improvement: Closely observe the performance of your global ad campaigns. Analyze essential metrics like reach, engagement, conversions, and ROI for each market. Regularly fine-tune your campaigns based on data insights to maximize results.

Local Alliances: Consider collaborating with local agencies or experts who have comprehensive knowledge about the specific markets you're targeting. They can offer valuable insights, assist with customization efforts, and help navigate cultural or regulatory obstacles.

Scheduling with Time Zones in Mind: Account for the time zone variations between your primary market and the international markets you're targeting. This ensures your content gets seen when your target audience is most likely to be active on TikTok.

Cultural Adaptation: Beyond language translation, focus on cultural nuances and preferences when modifying your ad content. Create content that resonates with the local audience.

Localized Trends and Hashtags: Utilize localized hashtags and participate in trending challenges that are popular in each market. This can help increase your ad visibility and relevance.

Adapting to Platform Usage: User behavior and content preferences may vary across regions. Adjust your ad strategies to align with how TikTok is used in each market.

Preliminary Testing: Prior to launching large-scale campaigns in international markets, consider conducting smaller-scale tests...